# Sledding Song

🎵 Sing to the tune of
"Here We Go 'Round the Mulberry Bush."

**By Maria Fleming**

Here we go marching through
the snow, through the snow,
through the snow.

Here we go marching
through the snow.
Winter is so much fun!

(3)

Here we go climbing up the hill,
up the hill, up the hill.

Here we go climbing up the hill.
Winter is so much fun!

(5)

Here we go sliding down the hill,
down the hill, down the hill.

Here we go sliding down the hill... ⑦

Winter is so much fun!